Aahana and the Two Brains

SECRET CODE TO POWER UP YOUR BRAIN — AND YOUR HEART.

JOIN AAHANA ON HER QUEST TO DISCOVER THE WORLD'S MOST MAGICAL MAP.

Avinash Parhi

This is a work of non fiction. The incidents in the book are inspired by real events. However, some names and characteristics have been changed, some events have been compressed, and some dialogues have been recreated. Any resemblance is purely coincidental.

First Edition: December 2025
Printed in India

Printed at: Thomson Press India Private Limited
Typeset in Libertinus Serif
ISBN: 978-93-6070-070-6

Cover Design: Prajakta Sawant

STORYMIRROR
Stories that reflect you

Publisher:	StoryMirror Infotech Pvt. Ltd. Unit No-F/705, 7th Floor, Kailas Corporate Lounge, Veer Savarkar Road, Vikhroli Park Site, Vikhroli West, Mumbai-400079, Maharashtra, India.
Web:	storymirror.com
Facebook:	@storymirror
Twitter:	@story_mirror
Instagram:	@storymirror
Email:	marketing@storymirror.com

*"Dedicated to my beloved daughter, Aahana,
whose curiosity, love for learning & our distance
inspired this work."*

Foreword

In a world that often teaches children how to succeed but rarely how to be, this book arrives like a breath of sincerity. What Avinash has written comes not from ambition, but from authenticity – from a genuine desire to shape young minds with wisdom that truly matters. These are not just stories or ideas; they are seeds of character, compassion, and curiosity. I believe every child – and every parent – who reads this will walk away a little more thoughtful, and a lot more human. What stayed with me as I read the chapters was the clarity with which Avinash translates the inner workings of a child's mind into simple, relatable experiences. The tug-of-war between fast impulses and slower wisdom, the idea of noticing thoughts before acting – these are concepts most adults discover late in life. Here, they are introduced with a lightness that children will instinctively understand.

As someone who has spent years writing about emotions, decisions, and the quiet battles people fight within themselves, I found this book refreshing. It respects the emotional intelligence of a young reader. It offers not just explanations, but small practices – reflection boxes, little missions, moments that invite a child to pause and understand themselves a bit better. The beauty of this book lies in how gently it teaches. Nothing is forced, nothing is loud. It shares tools children can carry as they grow, long after the story ends.

Books can entertain, but the meaningful ones stay. I believe this one will.

Ravinder Singh
Author of National Bestsellers

Words that Made Us Smile

Making choices and balancing options are difficult at any age. This wonderful book takes us through interesting discussions between a father and a daughter, this wonderful book shows us how to navigate through different contexts and make decisions.

Rukmini Banerji,
CEO - Pratham Education Foundation

Born from a father's love and refined through the voices of over 60 children, this book is both intimate and universal. 'Aahana and the Two Brains' is a tender, playful guide that gives children the language, courage, and clarity to understand their inner world. It feels less like a book and more like a map — helping young readers navigate emotions with humour, honesty, and heart.

Kiran Bir Sethi,
Founder, Riverside School & Design for Change

Aahana discovers real-life superpowers hidden inside her own mind, and Avinash turns that journey into a warm, magical guide for every growing child.

A simple, relatable adventure that helps kids understand feelings, choices and courage - one small moment at a time.

Ankur Warikoo,
Entrepreneur, Educator & Investor

This book is a gentle, intelligent reminder that children need support not only to learn, but to understand themselves. Through simple conversations and everyday dilemmas, the book helps young readers recognise their thoughts, feelings, and choices with greater clarity.

What stays with you is the respect it shows for a child's inner world. The ideas of the Fast and Slow Brain, the Focus Flashlight, and the small reflective pauses give children language for emotions they often struggle to express.

The activities at the end of each chapter make the learning personal – encouraging children to slow down, think, and respond rather than react. In a world full of noise and hurry, this book offers a quiet, reassuring space for children to build confidence, awareness, and kindness towards themselves.

Radhika Bharat Ram,
Jt. Vice Chairperson. The Shri Ram Schools

....

Aahana and the Two Brains turns complex emotions into simple, memorable stories. Avinash has taken ideas from neuroscience and made them so relatable that a child can see their thoughts, name their feelings, and choose better responses. As a coach, I see adults struggle with this every day – how powerful it is for a child to learn it early. A gentle, wise book for every family

Sandeep Kochhar,
Storyteller & Leadership Coach

....

When Avinash first sent me an early draft of Aahana and the Two Brains, my first thought was 'Wow'; and a close second was 'Where was this book when my kids were growing up'; followed by a third 'Hey, where was this book when I was growing up?' The humour, simplicity and engaging narrative are underpinned by research and wisdom that I am able to relate to from my own training and extensive reading in psychology. Avinash has clearly put great heart as well as thinking in this wonderful book - so whether you're looking to gift a fun stimulating book to a curious, young mind, or looking for ideas to engage with your kids in a fun, non-preachy manner that respects their own agency, this is the book for you.

Each short, simple chapter is rounded off nicely with exercises that help integrate the concepts as they unfold, so that both left and right brain work together around an idea. This is the sort of book that lets learning seep in through what is, in my view, the best, most organic way and sticky way to learn - that is, play!

Yashodhara Lal,
Author, Psychotherapist & Coach

....

Aahana and the two brains is a fantastic attempt by a dad to reach out to children through the lead actor, Aahana- his daughter. The supporting role of the two brains has been crafted beautifully and their innumerable attempts to coax, provoke and tempt Aahana to listen to them. By making the choices, Aahana experiences the power to take decisions. The activities at the end of the chapter are a good way to encourage the readers to reflect and action their thoughts.

Sapna Dimri,
Principal - Shri Ram Jr School, Aravali

....

Imagine having a secret map to the trickiest place in the world: your own mind. That is exactly what Avinash Parhi has given young readers in this delightful and deeply insightful book, Aahana and The Two Brains.

As an educator who has spent years championing brain-based, child-centric learning, I know that the most powerful tool a child can possess isn't a high IQ score, but emotional and cognitive awareness. This book is a gentle, playful, and utterly brilliant guide to exactly that.

We live in a world that moves at the speed of light. Children today are constantly pulled between instant gratification: the "Fast Aahana" of the sleepover and cookies and long-term goals and the "Slow Aahana" of the chess tournament. This internal tug-of-war is real, but until now, we haven't had such an engaging framework to help children understand it.

By introducing the concepts of "Fast Brain" and "Slow Brain" (a child-friendly interpretation of System 1 and System 2 thinking), the author hands children the ultimate tool: the power of The Pause. Aahana's journey shows that it's not about fighting your impulsive side; it's about listening to both voices and choosing which one gets to lead for a better outcome. This is a foundational life skill.

The magic doesn't stop with choices. The book extends this self-awareness to crucial areas like Focus, through the wonderful metaphor of the "Focus Flashlight" and Emotions - What Filled Aahana's Glass? , Balloon Of Anger .

Aahana is a regular girl from Gurgaon who has big feelings and sticky problems, making her instantly relatable. By watching her decode her feelings and her father admit his own "Fast Brain" moment (the cautionary tale of the 'Squeaky Shoes' , children learn a vital lesson: it's okay to be human, and even heroes learn.

This book is more than a story; it's an interactive workshop for self-regulation, packed with "Secret Codes," "Mini-missions," and "Magic Journal Pages". It empowers readers to become their own secret agents who can manage their feelings and master their decisions.

For every parent who has said, "Just focus!" or, "Why did you do that without thinking?", this book is the answer. It gives children the language and the framework to understand why their brain acts the way it does.

If you want your child to unlock their fullest potential, hand them this book, tell them the journey is theirs, and watch them discover their real superpower: the courage to understand their own mind

Dr. Swati Popat Vats,
President Podar Education Network, President, ECA

Preface for the Readers

Hey there, secret agent!

Jahnavi used to feel stuck.

Her brain confused her. Sometimes it made her blurt things out.

On other times, it stayed quiet when she really wanted to speak up.

She felt angry, nervous, and guilty and didn't know why.

And grown-ups? Their rules made zero sense.

But then... Jahnavi found something.

Not a magic wand.

Not a grown-up lecture.

A book. Yes – this *book*!

By reading about how Aahana figured it out, she discovered her two brains - the fast one and the slow one.

She learned to pause, choose, decode her feelings... and even (shhh) **outsmart her parents.**

This isn't just Jahnavi's story anymore.

It's yours.

Because,

Hidden in these pages are:

🧩 Secret codes in every chapter

💥 Mini-missions to unlock hidden powers

✍ Magic journal pages that show how your brain really works

Some parts will make you laugh.

Some might surprise you.

All of them will help you power up from the inside out.

Take a deep breath. Whisper the spell:

"Mind, open. Heart, steady. Ninja brain – let's go!"

Ready? Flip the page.

Your story begins now. 🚀 🚀

Contents

Meet Aahana

Growing up in Gurgaon, a buzzing city next to New Delhi, Aahana wasn't born with superpowers. She didn't have laser eyes or a magic wand. But she had something even better: the power, the courage and ability to understand her own mind.

She wasn't always like that.

Often, she used to get stuck in tricky choices, feel big emotions, and wish someone would just give her the answers, until she found the secret codes.

Now, when her brain gets messy or her heart feels heavy, Aahana listens.

She decodes.

She decides.

And this book?

It holds the same codes she found.

The rest of the story is hers – unless you decide to make it yours too!

Section 1

How Aahana's Brain Made Choices

Chapter 1

Meet Aahana's Two Brains

Aahana was stuck. Not in a deep, muddy puddle. Though Sara, her school friend, had dared her to jump into one yesterday (and Aahana almost had). Not stuck in a video game level. She was stuck in a decision— the kind that makes your brain go all noisy.

Her best friend, Riya, had invited Aahana to a sleepover at her house tonight. Sleepovers at Riya's were legendary— they usually involved building magnificent pillow forts, telling spooky stories (mostly made up by Sara, who would then get scared by her own tales), and Riya's mom's famous triple-chocolate-chip cookies.

But there was a catch. Tomorrow morning, bright and early, was the inter-school chess tournament. Aahana was the school champion, and she'd been practicing for weeks.

Inside her head, it felt like a noisy marketplace with two very loud voices shouting over each other.

Fast Aahana: "Go to the sleepover! It'll be SO MUCH FUN! Pillow forts! Cookies! Staying up late! You can't miss it!" This voice was bouncy, impatient, and always looking for the next exciting thing. It sounded a lot like Sara on a sugar rush.

💭 ***Slow Aahana:*** "But the tournament... You need to be sharp and rested. If you're tired, you won't play your best. Remember how much you want to win?" This voice was calmer, more thoughtful, and a little bit like Riya when she was explaining something important.

Aahana flopped onto her bed with a groan. "Ugh! Why is it so hard to choose? It feels like I have two different people living inside my head!"

Her father, who was passing by her room, chuckled from the doorway. "That's because, in a way, you do!"

Aahana sat bolt upright. "Wait... WHAT? Am I growing a second head? Is that why Sara keeps saying I'm an alien?"

Her father laughed, a warm, rumbly sound, and came to sit on the edge of her bed. "Not quite a second head, champ. But you do have two very important 'voices' or 'thinkers' in your brain that help you make decisions." He held up two fingers.

"Think of it like this," he began, his eyes twinkling. "There's 'Fast Aahana.' She's super quick, loves excitement, reacts instantly, and doesn't always stop to think things through. She's the one who shouts 'YES!' to ice cream before I even finish asking, or the one who decided to wear mismatched shoes to school last Tuesday because it felt 'adventurous'."

Aahana giggled, remembering her stripy sock and spotty shoe combination. Sara had dared her to do the shoes, and Fast Aahana had leaped at the challenge. "That sounds like me! Especially the ice cream part."

"Exactly!" her father said. "Fast Aahana is great for quick reactions, like catching a ball Sara suddenly throws at you, or when you instantly know the answer to a simple math problem. She's also where your gut feelings come from."

"Then there's 'Slow Aahana'," he continued, wiggling his second finger. "Slow Aahana is more careful. She thinks things through, weighs the pros and cons, considers the long-term consequences, and helps you make more deliberate, often smarter, choices. She's the one who reminds you to study for a test even if Sara is begging you to come out and try her new water pistol, or the one who helps you solve a tricky puzzle by looking at all the pieces."

Aahana frowned. "So... which one is right? Fast Aahana wants the sleepover, and Slow Aahana wants me to rest for the tournament. They can't both be right!"

Her father smiled. "That's the secret, Aahana. It's not about one being 'right' and the other 'wrong.' Both voices are important. Interestingly, both voices are coming from just one brain; however, it might feel otherwise—two different brains with very contrasting voices! The trick is to know when to listen to which voice, or how to make them work together for your long-term benefit. Sometimes Fast Aahana is helpful, like when you need to make a quick decision in a game. Other times, Slow Aahana is better, especially for big decisions that have important outcomes, like your chess tournament."

He tapped her nose. "Think about what really matters most to you tomorrow. And think about what might happen with each choice."

Aahana thought about it. Fast Aahana was still jumping up and down, imagining the fun at Riya's: the smell of cookies, the thrill of a new pillow fort design, and giggling with Riya and Sara. But then Slow Aahana painted a picture too: sitting at the chess table tomorrow, her mind clear, making smart moves, the thrill of saying "Checkmate!" and maybe, just maybe, bringing home the trophy. She also pictured how grumpy and unfocused she felt when she was really tired. Last time she'd stayed up too late before a match, she'd made a silly mistake and lost to Kabir, her friend who usually wasn't able to beat her.

"So, Fast Aahana is about what I want right now," Aahana said slowly, "and Slow Aahana is about what I want later, or what's more important in the bigger picture?"

"You've got it!" her father said, beaming. "Sometimes, what you want right now is perfectly fine – like having that ice cream. But other times, waiting or choosing the less 'fun' option can lead to a much bigger reward. It's about finding the balance."

That night, Aahana called Riya. "I really, really want to come to the sleepover," she said, "but I think Slow Aahana is right this time. I need to be ready for the tournament."

Riya, being Riya, understood. "No worries, Aahana! We'll have another sleepover soon. Go, win that trophy! Maybe Sara and I can be your official cheerleaders!"

Aahana went to bed early, feeling a sense of calm. Fast Aahana had grumbled a bit, but Slow Aahana felt satisfied.

And guess what?

The next day, Aahana played brilliantly in the tournament. Her mind was clear, her moves were strategic, and she won! Holding the shiny trophy, she felt a huge surge of pride. Later that afternoon, Riya and a very excited Sara came over, and they celebrated with a mini-party, complete with Aahana's mom's (almost as famous) lemonade and pakoras. She even had time to show Kabir the winning moves.

Aahana realized her father was right. She hadn't missed out on fun with her friends, and she had achieved her goal. She had listened to both voices, understood what each was offering, and then let Slow Aahana take the lead for the bigger goal. She had found her balance. And that felt like a real superpower.

"Nerve impulses travel at 270 mph—
faster than a Formula 1 car.

Yet somehow, picking a movie on Netflix still
takes 45 minutes."

Interactive Box

1. Riddle of the Voices:

I have no mouth, but I speak to you often.

One of me is quick and loves to soften,

The other is careful, steady, and slow.

To make the best choices, both you must know.

What am I?

2. Creative Exercise:

Your Own 'Fast Me' and 'Slow Me' Avatars!

Imagine your 'Fast You' and 'Slow You' are little characters living in your head.

Draw them! What do they look like? What clothes do they wear? Do they have any special symbols or accessories? (Maybe Fast You has rocket shoes, and Slow You has a magnifying glass and a thinking cap!)

Give them names! (Like Aahana's Fast Aahana and Slow Aahana).

Write down three things each of your characters loves to do or say.

3. Optional Visual Puzzle Idea:

A split image. On one side, a chaotic, brightly coloured scene representing "Fast Aahana's" desires (e.g., candy, games, jumping around). On the other side, a calm, organized scene representing "Slow Aahana's" suggestions (e.g., a book, a chess piece, a focused expression). The reader has to identify which items belong to which thinking style.

Superpower Reflection Journal Prompt:

Think about a choice you made recently. Which voice – your 'Fast You' or your 'Slow You' – was louder? How did the choice turn out? Next time you have a decision, how can you try to listen to both?

Riddle Answer:

Your two inner voices (Fast and Slow Thinking)

Chapter 2

The Focus Flashlight

Aahana slumped at her desk, a stormy cloud hovering over her head, much like the one Sara had tried to draw in art class last week (it had ended up looking more like a giant, lumpy potato). Her history textbook, usually full of interesting stories about ancient kings and queens, felt as heavy as Kabir's backpack after he'd stuffed it with his rock collection. The homework assignment – "Write three paragraphs about the challenges faced by early explorers" – seemed less like a task and more like a mountain she had to climb in flip-flops.

It wasn't that Aahana disliked history. Riya could make any historical event sound like an exciting adventure story. But today, Aahana's mind was a buzzing beehive of everything *but* early explorers.

Ping! Her tablet, lying innocently on the corner of her desk, lit up. A new message from Sara in their group chat: "GUESS WHAT?! Mom finally said yes to the treehouse project! Kabir, bring your best design ideas! Aahana, we need your amazing decorating skills! 🎉 🌳"

Aahana's fingers twitched. A treehouse! She could almost smell the sawdust and feel the thrill of climbing up high. Visions of fairy lights, comfy cushions, and a secret snack compartment danced in her head. "Just one peek at the chat," she told herself. "It'll only take a second."

Thirty minutes later, Aahana was deep into a debate with Sara about whether the treehouse should have a rope ladder or a spiral staircase (Sara was rooting for a zipline entrance, which Riya had gently pointed out might be a tad ambitious for their first build). The history textbook lay forgotten; explorers still facing their ancient challenges all alone.

With a jolt, Aahana remembered her homework. "Oh no!" she groaned, guilt washing over her. Why was it so hard to just do what she needed to do? Her brain felt like a pinball machine, thoughts bouncing wildly from one shiny distraction to another. She imagined her focus was a tiny, scared mouse, and the distractions were Sara's cat, Mittens, playfully (but effectively) chasing it all over the place.

Her father walked in, noticing her frustrated expression and the way she was glaring at the textbook as if it had personally offended her. "Explorer troubles, champ?" he asked, his voice kind.

“Dad, I just can’t focus!” Aahana wailed, throwing her hands up in the air. “My brain keeps running off to play. First, it was the treehouse messages; then I remembered I wanted to check if Taylor Swift announced new tour dates in India, and then I started wondering if Kabir has figured out that impossible level in his game yet. The explorers are still stuck in the Stone Age because of me!”

Her father chuckled, a warm sound that always made her feel a little better. “It sounds like your attention is having a party, and everyone’s invited except the explorers.” He picked up a small, powerful LED flashlight from her desk drawer, one she used for reading under the covers.

“Want to know a secret about focus?” he asked, his eyes twinkling. Aahana nodded, always ready for one of her dad’s secrets. They were usually much more interesting than the secrets Sara tried to share, which often involved who had a crush on whom or where she’d hidden Kabir’s favourite pen.

“Your brain,” her father said, switching on the flashlight, “is a lot like this flashlight.” He aimed the bright, concentrated beam at her history textbook. “Whatever you shine it on, that’s what you see clearly. Right now, this beam is just on your book. Can you see the picture of the old ship?”

Aahana nodded. The ship, moments ago a dull smudge, now looked detailed and interesting.

“Now,” he said, sweeping the flashlight beam quickly around the room – over her colourful posters, her messy craft corner, the window looking out onto the garden. “Try focusing on everything the beam touches all at once. The ship, the poster of the solar system, that half-finished painting of a rainbow unicorn Sara convinced you to start, the bird on the tree outside... Can you see them all with the same clarity as when the light was just on the ship?”

Aahana tried, her eyes darting around. "No," she admitted. "It's all a blur. I can sort of see things, but nothing is sharp. It's like the flashlight is trying to do too much."

"Exactly!" her father said. "Your brain works the same way. It can only truly focus its bright light on one main thing at a time. When you try to focus on your homework, the tablet, and your thoughts about the treehouse, your brain's flashlight beam is scattered, and nothing gets your full attention. It's like trying to light up a whole stadium with this one little flashlight."

Aahana looked at the flashlight, then at her textbook. "So, when I tell myself to focus on homework, I'm telling my brain to shine its flashlight only on the explorers?"

"You've got it," he grinned. "And when a distraction pops up – like a treehouse thought or a tablet notification – that's like someone trying to wiggle your flashlight and point it somewhere else. Your job is to gently, but firmly, guide the beam back to what you chose to focus on."

Aahana had an idea. She put her tablet on silent and placed it on her bookshelf, out of immediate reach. Then, she took a deep breath, closed her eyes for a second, and imagined she had a special 'Focus Flashlight' inside her head. She pictured its beam, strong and steady, shining directly onto the page about early explorers.

She started reading. A thought about the treehouse popped into her head. Nope, she thought, visualizing herself gently aiming her Focus Flashlight back to the words in the textbook. Explorers first, treehouse later. She imagined the explorers needed her focused light to find their way.

It wasn't easy at first. Aahana's mental flashlight still tried to flicker towards what Sara might be messaging, or whether Riya had already finished her homework (Riya probably had; she had a Focus Flashlight that could rival a lighthouse beam). But each time her mind wandered, Aahana pictured her flashlight and nudged it back. Slowly, the world of the early explorers started to come alive. She read about their creaking wooden ships, their fear of the unknown, and their excitement at discovering new lands.

An hour later, Aahana wrote the last sentence of her third paragraph. She stretched, a genuine smile spreading across her face. The mountain hadn't just been climbed; it had shrunk into a manageable hill! She hadn't just completed her homework; she actually felt like she'd learned something.

"Dad!" she called out, running into the living room. "The flashlight trick worked! The explorers have been successfully conquered!"

Her father looked up from his newspaper, a proud smile on his face. "See? You had the superpower of focus within you all along. You just needed to learn how to aim it."

Aahana realized that focus wasn't about forcing her brain to be quiet; it was about choosing where to shine her light. And that felt incredibly powerful, almost as powerful as Sara's determination to build a zipline. Maybe, just maybe, with her Focus Flashlight, she could even help Sara figure out the logistics of that zipline... after her other homework was done, of course.

"Goldfish attention span: 9 seconds.
Human attention span: 8 seconds.

You are officially losing to a fish.
Oh look! A squirrel!"

Interactive Box

1. Riddle of the Light:

I have no voice, but I help you learn and see.

The more you direct me, the sharper things will be.

If I scatter and stray, tasks take all day.

What am I?

2. Creative Exercise:

Design Your Distraction Dodgers!

Imagine those pesky thoughts or things that try to pull your Focus Flashlight away are little "Distraction Dodgers" or "Focus Snatchers."

Draw them! What do your personal Distraction Dodgers look like? Are they cute and sneaky, loud and bouncy, or sparkly and tempting (like a new game notification)? Give them funny names (e.g., The "Just One More Video" Viper, The "Daydream Dragon," The "Snack Siren").

Now, draw your Super Focus Flashlight! What makes it super? Does it have special power-ups? How does it gently shoo away the Distraction Dodgers and keep its beam strong on what's important? Maybe it has a "Gentle Return" button or a "Mute Distractions" shield!

3. Optional Visual Puzzle Idea:

Focus Maze!

Create a maze where the path is a beam of light from a flashlight at the start to a goal (like a completed homework book) at the end. Along the wrong paths, place drawings of common distractions (a game controller, a ringing phone, a thought bubble of friends playing). The player has to keep their pencil within the "beam of light" to reach the goal, sharpening their visual focus.

Superpower Reflection Journal Prompt:

Think about the last time you found it really hard to focus on something, like homework or listening to someone. What were your main "Distraction Dodgers" doing to pull your attention away? Next time you need to focus, how will you use your imaginary "Focus Flashlight" to stay on track? What will you tell your Dodgers?

Riddle Answer:

Your Focus (or your Focus Flashlight!)

Chapter 3

The Puzzle Trick

It was Kabir's birthday, and he'd received the most amazing present: a 1000-piece jigsaw puzzle of a scene from their favourite fantasy movie, "The Dragon's Cipher." It showed a knight, a princess, and a friendly-looking purple dragon soaring over a landscape filled with sparkling waterfalls and mysterious, glowing caves. When Kabir unrolled the poster-sized image, Aahana, Riya, and Sara gasped. It was beautiful, intricate, and looked incredibly... complicated.

"Wow, Kabir! This is epic!" Aahana exclaimed, her eyes wide.

"Let's do it! Let's do it now!" Sara bounced, already reaching for the box.

Riya, ever the planner, suggested, "We should clear the big table in the living room."

Soon, the four friends were gathered around the table, the thousand puzzle pieces spread out like a colourful, chaotic sea. The initial excitement was a fizzy drink, bubbling with energy. Sara, true to form, dived right in, grabbing random pieces and trying to jam them together, humming a tune that sounded suspiciously like a battle march. Kabir, being more methodical, started looking for pieces with bits of the purple dragon on them.

Riya was trying to find all the straight-edged border pieces. Aahana picked up a piece that was mostly blue sky and another that was a confusing swirl of green and brown.

An hour passed. The fizzy drink of excitement had gone completely flat. The table still looked like a mess of random pieces. They had managed to connect maybe ten pieces in total, and two of those Sara had forced together so hard they looked a bit bent.

"This is IMPOSSIBLE!" Aahana groaned, slumping back in her chair. "There are too many! They all look the same! We'll be here until we're old and grey, and the dragon will still be in a million bits!"

Sara, surprisingly, agreed. "My brain hurts. I think this puzzle is a secret trick to make us all go bonkers." She flopped dramatically onto the carpet.

Kabir sighed, his shoulders drooping. "I really wanted to see the dragon."

Even Riya looked a bit disheartened. "It's definitely harder than I thought."

Aahana's father walked in, carrying a tray with glasses of lemonade and a plate of cookies. He took in the scene: the dejected faces, the mountain of puzzle pieces, Sara looking like a defeated starfish on the floor.

"Looks like 'The Dragon's Cipher' is putting up a good fight, eh?" he said with a smile.

"Dad, it's not a fight, it's a disaster!" Aahana said. "This puzzle is just too big. We can't do it."

Her father set the tray down. "Hmm," he said, picking up a single puzzle piece. "A big task can feel like that sometimes. Like trying to eat a giant pizza in one bite. But what if I told you there's a trick to solving even the biggest, most complicated puzzles?"

Aahana, Riya, and Kabir looked up. Sara even lifted her head from the floor. "A trick? Like a magic spell?" she asked hopefully.

Her father chuckled. "Sort of a magic spell. It's called 'The Puzzle Trick'."

He sat down with them. "When you first look at all these pieces," he said, gesturing to the table, "it's overwhelming, right? Your brain doesn't know where to start. But what's the first thing you usually do with a puzzle, Riya?"

Riya perked up slightly. "Find the edge pieces?"

"Exactly!" he said. "Why do we do that?"

"Because it gives you a frame," Kabir offered. "It makes the space smaller."

"Precisely," her father said. "You're breaking the big problem – the whole puzzle – into a smaller, more manageable first step: complete the border. That's part one of The Puzzle Trick."

He continued, "What's next? Once the border is done, do you just randomly try to fill it in?"

Aahana thought about it. "No... you sort of look for colours, right? Or specific things in the picture. Like, all the blue sky pieces, or all the pieces that make up the dragon's purple scales."

"You got it!" her father said. "You sort the pieces into groups. Sky, dragon, waterfall, and castle. You're breaking the big picture down into smaller sections. Instead of trying to solve the whole 1000-piece puzzle at once, you're now solving a 50-piece sky puzzle, then a 70-piece dragon puzzle. Much easier, right?"

The friends looked at each other. It sounded so simple.

"So, the trick is to not look at the whole scary mountain of pieces," Aahana said slowly, "but to just focus on one small part at a time?"

“That’s the heart of it,” her father nodded. “Break big problems into smaller parts, and then tackle those smaller parts one by one. Each small success gives you a boost and makes the next part seem less daunting.”

Inspired, they decided to try again. With her father’s guidance, they first hunted down all the edge pieces. Sara, surprisingly, was very good at this, her eyes darting over the pieces like a treasure-hunting hawk. Soon, they had the entire border of “The Dragon’s Cipher” complete. It felt like a huge victory!

Then, they started sorting. Aahana took charge of the sky and waterfall pieces. Kabir, of course, claimed all the purple and scaly dragon pieces. Riya focused on the castle, and Sara decided to find all the pieces with any hint of red or orange, which she declared were “explosion and lava pieces” (even though there were no explosions or lava in the picture).

Slowly, magically, the picture began to emerge. A patch of sky here, a piece of the dragon’s wing there. Whenever Aahana felt a wave of “this is still too much!” she’d remind herself, “Just this section. Just the waterfall.” She realized her father was right.

Focusing on one small area made it feel like a mini-puzzle, fun and achievable.

Later that afternoon, as they were admiring a fully assembled shimmering waterfall, Aahana's father asked, "You know, this Puzzle Trick doesn't just work for jigsaw puzzles."

Aahana looked at him. "What do you mean?"

"Think about that big science project you have due next month," he said. "Does it feel a bit like this 1000-piece puzzle?"

Aahana's eyes widened. It did! The project, on 'Renewable Energy,' seemed huge and confusing.

"So, I could use The Puzzle Trick for that too?" she asked. "Break it into smaller pieces? Like, first, research different types of renewable energy. Then, choose one. Then, write the introduction..."

"Exactly!" her father smiled. "Researching is like finding the edge pieces. Choosing a topic is like sorting a colour group. Writing one section is like completing a small part of the picture. Before you know it, your 'impossible' project will be done." 👍

By the end of the day, the dragon wasn't fully complete, but they had made incredible progress. Large sections were finished, and everyone could see the magnificent creature taking shape. More importantly, the frustration was gone, replaced by a buzz of collaborative pride. Aahana looked at the half-finished puzzle, then at her friends, all happily chatting and fitting pieces. The Puzzle Trick wasn't just about jigsaws. It was about facing anything that seemed too big, too hard, or too scary, and knowing you could break it down and conquer it, one piece at a time. That felt like a real superpower.💪🔥

"Solving a big problem instantly is like trying to eat a watermelon in one bite.

It's messy, impossible, and someone is going to need a mop."

Interactive Box

1. Riddle of the Pieces:

I have many parts, but when I am whole, I tell a story or show a goal.

You solve me by looking, piece by piece, not all at once, for your mind to find peace.

What am I?

2. Creative Exercise:

Your Life-Sized Puzzle Plan!

Think of a big goal or a task in your life that feels a bit like a 1000-piece puzzle right now. It could be learning a new song on the piano, cleaning your whole room, getting better at a sport, or a big school assignment.

- ***Draw a giant, empty jigsaw puzzle shape*** on a piece of paper.
- ***Write your big goal in the middle of the puzzle shape.***
- ***Now, think about the smaller steps*** you need to take to achieve that goal. These are your individual puzzle pieces! Draw lines to divide your giant puzzle shape into 5-7 smaller pieces.
- ***In each smaller piece, write or draw one small, manageable step.*** For example, if your goal is "Clean My Room," a piece might be "Put all clothes in the laundry," another "Organize my desk," another "Make my bed."
- ***Colour in the first piece*** you will tackle! How does it feel to see your big goal broken down into a clear, step-by-step plan?

3. Optional Visual Puzzle Idea:

The Problem-Solving Maze!

Design a maze!

Start: Label the entrance of your maze "A Big Challenge!" (e.g., "Messy Room Mountain" or "Homework Headache").

End: Label the exit "Solved! Great Job!"

Pathways: The correct path through the maze should have little milestone markers or mini-goals written on it, like "Find Edge Pieces" -> "Sort by Colours" -> "Complete Small Section" -> "Take a Short Break" -> "Focus on Next Section."

Dead Ends: The dead ends can have little "Challenge Blockers" written in them, like "Feeling Overwhelmed," "Trying to do it all at once," or "Getting Distracted." The idea is to visually show that breaking a problem down (following the path with mini-goals) leads to the solution.

Superpower Reflection Journal Prompt:

Think about something you need to do that feels like a really big, complicated puzzle (like a school project, learning a new skill, or even a difficult conversation). What is the very first "edge piece" you can tackle? What are two or three "small sections" (or mini-tasks) you can focus on one at a time to make the whole thing feel less overwhelming and more achievable? Write them down!

Riddle Answer:

A jigsaw puzzle (or a big problem!)

Chapter 4

The Chocolate Confusion

Aahana loved Saturdays: no school, a chance to hang out with Riya, Kabir, and Sara, and often, her dad would have a little surprise or a fun activity planned. Today, however, the fun seemed to come with a very tricky test.

After lunch, her father called her into the kitchen. His eyes held that familiar mischievous twinkle that usually meant something interesting was about to happen. On the kitchen counter, he placed two small plates. On the first plate sat a single, shiny, perfectly wrapped chocolate coin – Aahana's favourite kind. Her mouth watered just looking at it. On the second plate, to her surprise, were three identical chocolate coins.

"All right, Aahana," her father said, his voice serious but with a smile playing on his lips. "Here's a little challenge for you. You have two choices. You can have this one chocolate coin right now." He pointed to the plate with the single coin. "Or..." he paused dramatically, "you can choose to wait for fifteen minutes, without touching this single coin, and if you manage that, you can have all three chocolate coins."

Aahana stared at the plates. One chocolate coin... now. Three chocolate coins... later.

Fifteen minutes! That felt like an eternity, especially with a delicious chocolate coin sitting right there, practically calling her name.

"That's... that's a tricky one, Dad!" Aahana said, feeling a familiar tug-of-war inside her head.

It was like Fast Aahana and Slow Aahana from her earlier dilemma were back, having a very loud debate.

Fast Aahana: "Chocolate! Right now! It's there! Why wait? Fifteen minutes is ages! What if a friendly chocolate-eating alien beams in and eats them all before then? Grab it! Quick!"

Slow Aahana: "Hmm, but three chocolates are definitely better than one. Fifteen minutes isn't that long if you think about it. Imagine how good three will taste. And Dad looks like he's testing something important."

"Why are you doing this, Dad?" Aahana asked, her eyes still glued to the single chocolate coin. "Is this some kind of new Saturday game?"🎮

Her father chuckled. "In a way, it is. It's a bit like a famous experiment scientists did a long time ago. They called it 'The Marshmallow Test.' They gave children a choice: one marshmallow now, or two marshmallows if they waited a little while."

"Marshmallows?" Aahana wrinkled her nose slightly. "Chocolate is way better. So, what happened with the marshmallow kids?"

"Well," her father continued, "the scientists found something really interesting. The children who were able to wait for the bigger reward – the two marshmallows – often grew up to be more successful in different parts of their lives. It wasn't just about marshmallows, of course. It showed that they were good at being patient and making choices that would benefit them more in the long run."

Patience. Long-term rewards. Aahana thought about it. She really wanted that one chocolate now. Fast Aahana was practically jumping up and down, shouting, "EAT IT! EAT IT!" But the idea of three chocolates, and the thought that waiting could be a kind of superpower, made Slow Aahana nod thoughtfully.

"Okay, Dad," Aahana said, taking a deep breath. "I'll try. I'll wait for the three chocolates."

"Excellent choice to make," her father said, smiling. He set a little kitchen timer for fifteen minutes. "You can stay here, or you can go play in your room, whatever helps you wait."

Aahana decided staying in the kitchen, staring at the chocolate, would be actual torture. She went to her room. But the chocolate coin followed her in her thoughts. She tried reading, but the words kept blurring into chocolatey shapes. She thought about calling Sara, but Sara would probably tell her to just eat the chocolate and then try to convince her dad to give her the other two anyway because "sharing is caring, especially when it's about chocolate destined for Sara's tummy."

She remembered the flashlight trick her dad had taught her for focus. Maybe she could use that here? What if she focused her flashlight on something else? She spotted her piggy bank on her shelf. She'd been saving up for a new advanced art kit Riya had told her about. It was expensive, and it felt like it would take forever to save enough. Every week, when she got her small pocket money, Fast Aahana would urge her to buy a small toy or some stickers. But Slow Aahana would whisper about the amazing art kit. Saving for the art kit was like waiting for the three chocolate coins, but on a much bigger scale.

For the next ten minutes, Aahana took out all her saved money, counted it, and then drew a picture of the art kit, imagining all the cool things she could create with it. She got so lost in her drawing and dreaming that when the timer buzzed loudly from the kitchen, it made her jump.

Fifteen minutes had passed!

She hurried back to the kitchen. Her father was there, a proud smile on his face. The single chocolate coin was still on its plate, untouched. And next to it, the plate with three chocolate coins seemed to sparkle even more.

"You did it!" her father said. "How does it feel?"

"It was hard!" Aahana admitted. "But... it also feels really good. Like I won a secret battle against my own jumpy brain!"

She carefully took the plate with the three chocolate coins. They tasted extra delicious.

Later that day, Aahana was playing a game with Kabir. Kabir was learning a new, complicated strategy in chess that required a lot of patient setup. He kept getting frustrated when his initial moves didn't lead to an immediate advantage.

"It's like Dad's chocolate test, Kabir," Aahana found herself saying. "Sometimes you have to make small, patient moves now to win big later. Short-term thinking wants to attack right away, but long-term thinking builds a stronger position."

Kabir looked at her, then at the chessboard. "Huh. Never thought of it that way. So, this boring pawn move is like... not eating the chocolate right away?"

Aahana grinned. "Exactly! And checkmate later will be like getting three chocolates!"

Aahana realized that this "short-term versus long-term" thinking was everywhere: finishing her homework before going out to play with Sara (short-term pain for long-term fun without worry); practicing her new song on the keyboard even when she fumbled (short-term effort for the long-term joy of playing it perfectly). Even Riya's careful planning for their group projects was a form of long-term thinking.

Waiting wasn't just about being bored or holding back. It was about choosing a bigger, better future for herself, one chocolate coin, one saved rupee, one patient chess move at a time. And that, Aahana decided, was a pretty sweet superpower to have.

"Time is weird.

5 minutes of gaming feels like 5 seconds. But 5 minutes of waiting for pizza? That feels like 500 years."

Interactive Box

1. Riddles About Patience:

1. I am a virtue, quiet and slow. If you have me, good things will grow. Rushing and hurrying make me depart. What am I, a treasure of the heart?
2. I have no hands, but I can help you wait. I'm not a clock, but I can conquer fate. The more you use me when things feel delayed, The bigger the prize that will come your way. What am I?

2. Creative Exercise:

My "Worth the Wait" Jar!

Think about something you really want that takes time to achieve or save up for (like a special toy, a new skill, a future holiday, or even a good grade in a tough subject).

- Find an old, clean jar (or draw a big one on paper).
- Decorate it and label it "My Worth the Wait Jar for [Your Goal]"
- On small slips of paper, write down:
- Why this goal is important to you.
- The good feelings you'll have when you achieve it.
- Small steps you can take along the way to work towards it.
- Things you can do to make the waiting time more enjoyable or productive (like Aahana distracting herself by thinking about her art kit).
- Every time you feel impatient, or when Fast You wants to give up on the long-term goal for something instant, take out a slip from your jar and read it to remind yourself why it's worth the wait!

3. Optional Visual Puzzle Idea:

The Problem-Solving Maze!

Create a simple board game path leading from "Start (Small Treat Now!)" to "Finish (Big Reward Later!)." The path should have various squares. Some could be "Temptation! You want to give up and take the small treat. Go back 2 spaces!" Other squares could be "Patience Power! You find a fun way to wait. Move forward 3 spaces!" or "Focused on the Goal! You remember why you're waiting. Move forward 1 space!" The visual would reinforce that while there are setbacks (temptations), acts of patience move you closer to the bigger reward. You could even add little pictures of "small treats" vs. the "big reward."

Superpower Reflection Journal Prompt:

Think about a time you chose a small, quick reward instead of waiting for a bigger one. How did that feel afterwards? Now, think of something you are currently waiting for or working towards patiently (like saving for a toy, learning a new song, or waiting for a special event). What does your 'Fast You' say about the waiting? What can your 'Slow You' remind you about why the bigger, long-term reward will be worth it?

Riddle Answer:

1. Patience

2. Patience

Chapter 5

The Whispering Coins

Aahana stared at her weekly planner, a frown creasing her forehead. This Saturday presented a classic Aahana-level dilemma, the kind that made her brain feel like a tangled ball of yarn.

On one hand, Riya had invited her, Sara, and Kabir for a special early screening of "Galaxy Guardians 3: The Nebula's Secret." They had been waiting for this movie for months! There would be popcorn, Sara's hilarious running commentary (whispered, of course, Riya would make sure of that), and endless discussions afterwards about their favourite alien creatures and plot twists. It was prime friend-time, guaranteed fun.

On the other hand, her father had excitedly told her about the "Innovators' Science Fair" happening on the very same Saturday afternoon. It was a huge event, showcasing amazing inventions by students, cool robotics demonstrations, and even a chance to try out some virtual reality experiences. Kabir was already planning to go with his older sister, and he'd been buzzing about a rumoured life-sized model of the Mars Rover. Aahana loved science, and the fair sounded incredibly cool and inspiring.

"Uggggh!" Aahana groaned, dropping her head onto her planner. "Why do good things always happen at the exact same time?" It was like the universe was playing a prank on her. Movie night with her best friends Or...Awesome science fair with her dad and potentially Kabir. Both sounded fantastic. Both felt unmissable.

Fast Aahana was doing energetic cartwheels, imagining the thrill of the movie's special effects. Slow Aahana was meticulously picturing the fascinating exhibits at the science fair. For once, they weren't arguing against each other; they were both just shouting "YES!" but for different things, making the decision even harder.

Her father walked past and saw her looking utterly dejected, a state usually reserved for when her favourite ice cream flavour was sold out. "Big decision brewing, champ?" he asked, his voice gentle.

"The biggest!" Aahana sighed. "It's Galaxy Guardians 3 versus the Innovators' Science Fair. How can anyone choose? What if I pick the wrong one and miss out on something amazing?" The dreaded FOMO – Fear Of Missing Out – was starting to bubble up.

Her father sat down beside her. "Ah, the classic dilemma of two wonderful choices. It's like having to pick between two equally delicious flavours of kulfi, isn't it? Sometimes, when your head is spinning with pros and cons, you need a little trick to hear what your heart is truly leaning towards." He pulled a shiny ten-rupee coin from his pocket. "Ever heard of the 'Whispering Coin' trick?"

Aahana looked up, intrigued. "A whispering coin? Does it actually talk?" Sara would love that.♥♥

Her father chuckled. "Not out loud, but it can help you hear your own whispers. Here's how it works. You assign one choice to 'Heads' and the other to 'Tails'." He handed her the coin. "Let's say, Heads for Galaxy Guardians, and Tails for the Science Fair."

Aahana nodded, holding the cool metal in her palm.

"Now," her father continued, his voice dropping to a conspiratorial whisper, "you're going to flip the coin. But here's the crucial part: as the coin is spinning in the air, I want you to pay very close attention to one tiny feeling. What are you hoping it will land on? Not what you think it should be, or what would make others happy, but what your gut, your heart, is secretly wishing for in that split second."

Aahana was skeptical. "So, the coin doesn't actually decide for me?"

"Nope," her father said. "The coin is just a helper. It creates a tiny moment of suspense. And in that moment, your true preference often reveals itself like a quick whisper. What you hope for while it's in the air is usually what you wanted deep down all along, even if your logical brain was busy arguing for both sides."

Aahana decided to try. It couldn't make things any worse.

"Okay," she said. "Heads for the movie, Tails for the science fair."

She took a deep breath, and with a flick of her thumb, sent the coin spinning upwards. It glinted in the light, turning over and over.

For a split second, as it hung in the air before starting its descent, a clear thought, a strong feeling, flashed through Aahana's mind: Oh, I really hope it's Tails!

The coin landed in her open palm. She covered it with her other hand, her heart beating a little faster. Slowly, she peeked.

It was Heads. Movie night.

But Aahana wasn't disappointed. In fact, she felt a strange sense of clarity. The moment the coin was in the air, that tiny, powerful wish for 'Tails' – for the science fair – had been so clear, so undeniable.

She looked up at her father, a slow smile spreading across her face. "Wow," she whispered. "It actually worked. I… I was hoping for Tails."

Her father grinned. "See? The Whispering Coin doesn't make the decision; it helps you discover the decision you've already made in your heart. Your head might have been tied in knots, but your heart knew."

"So even though it landed on Heads," Aahana mused, "I know I actually want to go to the science fair more?"

"Exactly!" her father confirmed. "Your fleeting hope for Tails was your intuition, your inner Aahana, telling you what would bring you a little more joy or fulfillment this particular Saturday. Now you can make your choice with more confidence."

Aahana felt a wave of relief wash over her. The tangled ball of yarn in her brain seemed to magically unsnarl. She did want to go to the science fair. The movie was going to be amazing, yes, but the thought of the new inventions and the Mars Rover model sparked a different kind of excitement in her, a curiosity that felt stronger right now.

She called Riya and explained. "I tried this cool coin trick, and it turns out I'm really leaning towards the science fair this weekend. But can we PLEASE plan a Galaxy Guardians movie marathon next weekend? We can even invite Kabir!"

Riya, being the wonderful friend she was, completely understood. "The science fair sounds awesome, Aahana! And a movie marathon next weekend is a brilliant idea! Sara will be thrilled – more time for her commentary!"

Later that day, Aahana thought about the Whispering Coin. It wasn't magic, not really. But it felt magical how it could cut through all the noise in her head and let her hear that quiet, true voice inside. She decided it was a superpower she could use for other tricky little choices too, like which book to read next from her towering pile, or even which flavour of kulfi to pick when both sounded equally delicious. The coin didn't hold the answers, but it definitely helped her find her own.

"Decisions are hard.

If you ever get stuck between pizza and a burger, remember: ' Bur-zza' isn't a thing yet... but you could be the inventor."

Interactive Box

1. Riddle of the Two Faces:

I have two faces but wear no disguise,

I speak no words, yet can make you wise.

When choices confuse and your mind is a haze,

A flip of me reveals your heart's true maze (and its exit)!

What am I?

2. Creative Exercise:

My Decision Compass!

Sometimes, even for small choices, our head says one thing and our heart whispers another! Let's practice listening to those whispers.

Think about a small, fun decision you might face:

- What game to play: A board game or an outdoor game?
- What to draw: Animals or a fantasy landscape?
- What after-school snack to pick: Fruit or a cookie?

For one of these (or a choice of your own):

1. Assign Option 1 to "Heads" and Option 2 to "Tails."
2. Close your eyes and imagine you're about to flip a coin. Really picture it spinning.
3. What are you secretly hoping for, even just a little bit, as it spins? This is your "Heart's Whisper."
4. Draw two columns. In one, write "My Head Says..." and list logical reasons for both choices. In the other, write "My Heart Whispered..." and note down what you hoped for.
5. How does it feel to notice that little whisper? Does it make the choice clearer or easier?

3. Optional Visual Puzzle Idea:

The Coin-Flip Decision-Making Game!

[This fulfills the "Coin-flip decision-making game" mentioned in the new contents page.]

Create a simple printable page with 3-4 scenarios like these:

Scenario 1: Weekend Fun!

- Heads: Go to the park with your bike.
- Tails: Build a massive fort in the living room.
- When you imagine flipping the coin, what do you secretly hope for? ___________

Scenario 2: Creative Time!

- Heads: Write a short story about a talking animal.
- Tails: Learn a new magic trick to show your family.
- When you imagine flipping the coin, what do you secretly hope for? ___________

Scenario 3: Helping Hand!

- Heads: Help your parent make dinner.
- Tails: Help a sibling with their homework.
- When you imagine flipping the coin, what do you secretly hope for? ___________

The game isn't about getting the "right" answer from the coin, but is for the child to practice noticing their internal preference (the "hope") for each scenario. They can write or draw their "hope."

Superpower Reflection Journal Prompt:

Think about a choice you have to make soon, big or small, where you feel a bit stuck between two options. Try the Whispering Coin trick: assign each option to Heads or Tails. When you (really or imaginarily) flip the coin, what tiny wish or hope do you feel while it's in the air? What did your heart whisper to you? Does this help you understand what you truly want, even a little bit more?

Riddle Answer:

A coin (when used for the Whispering Coin trick)

Section 2

How Aahana Felt Things Deep Inside

Chapter 6

What Filled Aahana's Glass?

Aahana slammed her bedroom door, the sound echoing her stormy mood. It had been a thoroughly rotten afternoon. First, Riya had seemed distracted and a bit dismissive when Aahana tried to share an exciting idea for their school science project. Then, during their group study session, Kabir had made a joke about her slightly mismatched socks (a daring Sara-inspired fashion choice Aahana had been proud of that morning), and Sara, instead of backing her up, had giggled along.

Now, at dinner, her mom had cheerfully served everyone's favourite lentil soup, alongside a small bowl of karela – bitter gourd – which Aahana usually didn't mind too much. But tonight, the sight of the pale green vegetable made her explode.

"Karela? Again?" she'd snapped, pushing her plate away. "Why do we always have to eat things I hate? This is the worst dinner ever!"

Her mother looked surprised by her outburst. "Aahana, you ate it just last week and said it was okay. And it's just a small side dish. What's really going on, sweetie?"

Aahana grumbled, "Nothing! I just hate karela, and my whole day has been awful, and now this!" She felt tears pricking her eyes, which was ridiculous. Crying over bitter gourd?

Later, after Aahana had calmed down a little (and eaten her soup, pointedly ignoring the karela), her mother came into her room. She was holding a glass of water.

“Feeling a bit better?” she asked gently.

Aahana shrugged, still feeling a knot of unhappiness in her tummy.

“You know, Aahana,” her mother said, sitting beside her. “Sometimes our feelings are like this glass of water.” She held it up. “Imagine this water is the grumpy mood you’ve been carrying around. Now, if I accidentally nudge this table, or if someone bumps into me while I’m holding it...” She gently shook the glass, and a little water sloshed over the side.

“The water spills, obviously,” Aahana said.

“Exactly,” her mother replied. “But why did it spill? Did the shaking create the water?”

Aahana frowned. “No, the water was already in the glass.”

"Precisely!" her mother said, her eyes kind. "The shaking, the little bump, just revealed what was already inside. It didn't put the water there. Sometimes, a small thing – like seeing karela on your plate when you're already feeling upset – isn't the real reason for a big emotional spill. It's just the little 'shake' that makes the feelings you're already carrying inside come tumbling out."

Aahana thought about this. The karela hadn't made her feel this awful. It was more like the final straw.

"So," she said slowly, "the karela was just the 'shake'?"

"It could be," her mother nodded. "Think about your day. Was there something earlier that might have 'filled your glass' with unhappy or angry feelings?"

Aahana's mind replayed the afternoon: Riya's distant replies and Kabir and Sara's laughter about her socks. Suddenly, it clicked. She hadn't been angry about the socks themselves – Fast Aahana had thought they were fun! But Kabir's joke, and especially Sara laughing with him, had made her feel... small. And a bit embarrassed. And Riya's earlier coolness had made her feel unimportant. That was the real source of the grumpy, heavy feeling. The karela had just been an easy target for her already full emotional glass.

"Oh," Aahana whispered, a wave of understanding washing over her. "I think... I was already upset because of what happened with Riya, Kabir, and Sara this afternoon. It made me feel a bit silly and left out."

Her mother gave her a hug. "See? Once you understand the real trigger, the real reason your 'glass was full,' the karela doesn't seem so powerful anymore, does it?"

Aahana shook her head. It really didn't. The knot in her tummy began to loosen.

"Knowing your triggers, sweetheart, is a real superpower," her mother said softly. "It helps you understand yourself better, and it means you don't always have to spill your 'water' when small things shake you."

That night, Aahana thought about her emotional glass. She decided she'd try to notice what filled it up during the day. Maybe if she understood her triggers, she could deal with the real feelings before they sloshed out over innocent vegetables. And perhaps, she'd even talk to Riya, Kabir, and Sara about how she'd felt. Understanding her own feelings was the first step.

"Bottling up feelings is exactly like shaking a warm soda.

Everything looks fine on the outside... until you open! KA-BOOM. Sticky explosion everywhere."

Interactive Box

1. Riddle of the Hidden Cause:

I am the spark that you might not see,

That makes a small problem feel big to thee.

You might blame the rain or a misplaced shoe,

But I'm the real reason you're feeling blue.

What am I?

2. Creative Exercise:

My "What's in My Glass?" Detector!

Imagine your emotions for the day are like water filling up a glass.

- Draw a tall, empty glass.
- Think about your day so far, or yesterday. What little things happened that might have added some "water" (feelings like frustration, sadness, annoyance, or even excitement that later made a small disappointment feel bigger) to your glass?
- For each one, draw a small symbol or write a word inside the glass representing that feeling or event (e.g., a little storm cloud for an argument, a deflated balloon for a disappointment, a question mark for confusion).
- Now, if a small thing happened later (the "shake"), like you couldn't find your favourite toy, how full was your glass already? Did understanding this help you see why your reaction might have been big or small?

3. Optional Visual Puzzle Idea:

Trigger Trails

Create a visual with a character (e.g., Aahana) showing a big emotional reaction to a very minor event in the foreground (e.g., dropping an ice cream). In the background, draw three or four little "event vignettes" that happened earlier in the day (e.g., an argument with a friend, a difficult test, not being picked for a game). The child has to draw a "trail" from the most likely earlier event (the main trigger) that contributed most to the big emotional reaction about the ice cream.

Superpower Reflection Journal Prompt:

Think about the last time you had a surprisingly big emotional reaction to something that seemed quite small. Take a moment, like Aahana did, to think about what else had happened earlier that day or the day before. Could there have been a hidden "trigger" – a different event or feeling – that had already 'filled up your emotional glass'? What was it? How does recognizing that trigger help you understand your reaction a little better?

Riddle Answer:

An emotional trigger

Chapter 7

Balloon of Anger

Aahana's fists were clenched so tight, her knuckles were white. Sara, in a whirlwind of enthusiastic but clumsy excitement while trying to show Aahana a new dance move she'd invented called, "The Wobbly Rainbow," had accidentally knocked Aahana's carefully built model of a futuristic city – her entry for the school's "Future Design" competition – right off the table. It had shattered into a dozen pieces.

Worse still, Sara's immediate reaction hadn't been a very sorry one. "Oops! Wow, it really flew! Don't worry, Aahana, we can just, like, call it 'Exploded City Chic'!" she'd said, giggling a little, clearly not understanding how many hours Aahana had poured into it.

Aahana felt a hot surge of anger rise up from her chest, so intense it almost choked her. She wanted to scream. She wanted to tell Sara she was the clumsiest, most thoughtless person in the world. But instead, she just bit her lip, turned her back, and seethed.

The anger didn't go away. It sat in her stomach like a hot coal. Every time she thought of Sara's careless laugh and her ruined model, she felt another puff of hot air swell inside her. She tried to ignore it, to think about other things, but the anger was a stubborn, heavy weight. She snapped at Kabir when he asked if she wanted to play their online game later and gave Riya a one-word answer when she called to chat.

Her father found her later, staring glumly at the broken pieces of her model, her face set in a stony mask. "Tough break with the model, champ," he said softly. "I saw Sara heading home, looking a bit like a deflated Wobbly Rainbow herself. She might be feeling worse than she let on."

Aahana just grunted. "She ruined it. And she didn't even care."

Her father nodded slowly. "Anger is a tricky thing, isn't it? It can feel so big and powerful." He then smiled a little. "I have an idea. How about a little experiment? Fetch me that packet of balloons from the craft drawer."

Puzzled, Aahana brought the balloons. Her father picked out a bright red one.

"This red balloon," he said, "is like your anger. Now, think about what Sara did, how it made you feel. For every wave of anger, blow some air into the balloon."

Aahana thought of her beautiful, intricate city, now just a pile of plastic rubble. Puff! She blew into the balloon.

She thought of Sara's silly giggle. Puff! Puff! The balloon grew.

She thought of all the hours she'd spent, now wasted. PUFF! PUFF! PUFF! The balloon swelled, becoming bigger and tighter, the red plastic stretched thin.

"Keep going," her father urged gently. "All that anger you're holding inside."

Aahana blew again, her cheeks aching. The balloon was now huge, taut, and trembling in her hands. It felt like it was about to explode.

"How does it feel to hold onto that, Aahana?" her father asked. "All that anger, packed so tightly."

"It's... it's really tense," Aahana managed, her hands gripping the balloon hard. "And it feels like it's going to burst any second! It's uncomfortable."

"Exactly," her father said. "That's what happens when we hold onto anger without letting it out. It builds and builds, making us tense and uncomfortable, and, eventually, it might just burst out in a way that isn't helpful – like yelling, saying hurtful things, or even breaking something else. That's the anger exploding, and it can make a mess."

He paused. "Now, what if, instead of letting it burst or holding on until it hurts, you tried to let the air out... very, very slowly?"

Aahana looked at the overinflated balloon. Carefully, she pinched the neck and allowed a tiny bit of air to escape. Hisssss.

The balloon deflated a little. It was still big, but not quite as dangerously tight.

"That's one way," her father said. "Sometimes, letting out a little bit of the pressure helps. But the best way to deal with the anger balloon is to find a healthy way to release the feeling that caused it in the first place, before it gets this big."

They talked about what that meant. It wasn't about pretending she wasn't angry. Anger was a normal feeling, like Joy or Sadness. But it was about what she did with it. Yelling at Sara might make her anger balloon burst, but it wouldn't fix her model or her feelings.

"Maybe," her father suggested, "you could tell Sara calmly how much the model meant to you, and how her reaction made you feel."

Later that evening, Aahana saw Sara sitting alone on her porch steps, looking unusually quiet. Aahana took a deep breath, remembering the taut red balloon. She walked over.

"Sara," she began, her voice a little shaky but calm. "I was really, really upset about my model. I spent so long on it. And when you laughed, it made me feel like you didn't understand or care how much it mattered to me."

Sara looked up, her eyes wide. "Oh, Aahana, I'm SO sorry! I didn't mean to laugh like that! I just... I get nervous and say silly things when I mess up. I felt awful as soon as it happened. Your model was amazing! Is there anything I can do to help fix it? I'm really good at finding tiny pieces!"

Hearing Sara's genuine apology and offer to help, Aahana felt that tight, uncomfortable pressure inside her chest start to ease, just like the air slowly hissing out of the balloon. It wasn't all gone, but it was so much lighter.

"Thanks, Sara," Aahana said, a small smile returning to her face. "Maybe we can try to fix it together tomorrow."

As she walked home, Aahana thought about her anger balloon. It wasn't about never feeling angry. It was about learning how to let the air out gently before it took over. And that, she realized, was much better than waiting for an explosion.

"Anger is like a sneeze.

If you hold it in, your whole head feels weird. Better to let it out—just not on someone's face."

Interactive Box

Riddle of the Hot Air:

I start as a spark when things go wrong,

If you bottle me up, I grow very strong.

I can make you red and ready to pop,

But a healthy release will make the pressure stop.

What am I?

2. Creative Exercise:

My Anger "Release Valves"!

Imagine your anger is like steam building up in a machine. If there's no way for the steam to get out, the machine might break! You need "release valves."

- Draw a picture of yourself feeling a little bit angry (maybe just some steam coming out of your ears!).
- Around your picture, draw 3-4 different-shaped "Release Valves."
- Inside each valve, write or draw a healthy thing you can do to let out your anger or frustration safely when you start to feel it build. Examples:
- "Talk to a grown-up or friend."
- "Squeeze a stress ball (or pillow)."
- "Write down why I'm angry."
- "Do 10 star jumps."
- "Listen to my favourite upbeat song."
- "Take slow, deep breaths."

3. Optional Visual Puzzle Idea:

The Anger Escalator/Stairs

Draw a simple escalator or a flight of stairs.

- At the bottom: "A small annoyance."
- Each step up represents escalating anger: "Feeling frustrated," "Getting really mad," "About to explode!"
- At the top (if no healthy release is chosen): "Anger Explosion! (Yelling, saying mean things)"
- Alongside the stairs, at different levels, draw "Release Options" or "Exit Ramps" (like "Take a deep breath," "Talk it out," "Walk away for a bit"). The child can draw a line showing how using a "Release Option" helps them get off the escalator before it reaches the "Explosion."

Superpower Reflection Journal Prompt:

Think about the last time you felt really angry – like your "anger balloon" was getting very full. What did you do with that feeling? Did you hold it in, or did it burst out? Imagine you could have used one of your "Anger Release Valves" (like talking calmly, taking deep breaths, or walking away for a minute). Which one would you have chosen, and how do you think it might have changed the situation or how you felt?

Riddle Answer:

Anger (like an overinflated balloon)

Chapter 8

Empathy Treasure Hunt

Aahana prided herself on being a good friend, but sometimes, she just didn't get why people got so upset over little things. Like today, her younger cousin, six-year-old Vivaan, was visiting, and he was in the middle of a full-blown meltdown because his favourite - small, slightly battered blue - race car had lost a wheel. Tears streamed down his face, and he let out wails that could rival a siren.

"Oh, come on, Vivaan," Aahana said, a little impatiently. She was trying to read a new adventure book Riya had loaned her. "It's just an old toy car. We can find another one. Stop making such a fuss."

Vivaan only cried harder, clutching the three-wheeled car to his chest as if it were the most precious treasure in the world.

Her father, who was in the adjoining room, overheard Aahana. He came into the living room, a thoughtful expression on his face. "That's a lot of sadness for one little car, isn't it?" he said, looking at Vivaan with kindness before turning to Aahana. "It can be puzzling when someone's feelings seem much bigger than the problem, Aahana."

He then winked. "What if I told you there's a hidden superpower that can help you understand these puzzling feelings? It's like going on an 'Empathy Treasure Hunt'."

Aahana was intrigued. "Empathy? Treasure Hunt?"

"Exactly," her father said. "Empathy is the ability to understand and share what someone else is feeling. It's like trying to see the world through their eyes for a moment. Sometimes, to find that treasure of understanding, you need to look for clues."

He picked up an old pair of his reading glasses from the side table. "Imagine these are special 'empathy glasses'," he said, handing them to Aahana. She put them on; they were a bit blurry.

"Now, looking at Vivaan through these 'blurry Vivaan-glasses,' can you see more than just a broken toy?"

Her father prompted gently, "To you, it's an old car. But what clues can you find about what this car means to Vivaan? When did he get it? Who gave it to him? What adventures has he had with it?"

Aahana looked at her little cousin, really looked this time. She remembered Vivaan had gotten that blue car from their grandfather, who lived far away and whom they didn't see very often. Vivaan took that car everywhere. He'd even made a little shoebox garage for it. It wasn't just any old toy; it was a piece of his connection to Grandpa, a companion in his imaginary races. The blurriness of her father's glasses seemed to represent how she hadn't seen all that before.

Suddenly, Aahana remembered a time when she was much younger. Her own beloved, scruffy teddy bear, Barnaby, had lost an eye. Her older cousins had teased her for crying over an "old, tatty bear." But Barnaby had been her confidant, her bedtime buddy. The feeling of loss had been huge.

Looking at Vivaan, she felt a pang of understanding. "Oh," she said softly, taking off the glasses. "It's not just a toy to him. It's his special car from Grandpa."

She went over to Vivaan and sat beside him. "I'm so sorry your blue car is broken, Vi," she said gently. "I know it's your favourite, the one Grandpa gave you."

Vivaan looked up, his sobs quieting a little. He nodded, tears still glistening on his cheeks.

"Remember when my Barnaby lost an eye?" Aahana continued. "I was so sad. I bet you feel a bit like that."

Vivaan nodded again, leaning his head against her arm.

"Maybe," Aahana suggested, "we can try to be car doctors. We can look for a new wheel, or maybe Dad can help us glue it back on very carefully."

A small glimmer of hope appeared in Vivaan's eyes.

Later, after a delicate operation involving superglue and a wheel from a less-loved toy truck (with Vivaan's solemn permission), the blue car was almost as good as new. Vivaan was beaming.

Aahana felt a warmth spread through her. It wasn't just the satisfaction of fixing the car; it was the good feeling of having understood and connected with her cousin. The "Empathy Treasure Hunt" had led her to something more valuable than gold.

The next day at school, during lunch, Sara was unusually quiet and wasn't eating her favourite pizza pockets. Normally, Aahana might have just shrugged it off, figuring Sara was just in a mood. But today, she remembered the empathy glasses. She decided to look for clues. Sara kept glancing at the noticeboard where the cast list for the school play had been posted that morning. Aahana knew Sara had auditioned for the lead role of the quirky detective.

Instead of just asking "What's wrong?", Aahana said gently, "Hey Sara, I saw you looking at the cast list for the play. Is everything okay?"

Sara sighed. "I didn't get the part I wanted. I'm just a 'Villager Number 3'."

Aahana could hear the disappointment in her voice. "Oh, Sara, that's tough. I know how much you wanted that detective role. It's okay to feel bummed out."

Sara gave her a small, grateful smile. "Thanks, Aahana. Yeah, it kind of stinks."

They talked for a bit longer, and Aahana just listened, offering a supportive word here and there. She didn't try to fix it, just to understand. And she could tell it helped Sara feel a little less alone with her disappointment.

Empathy, Aahana decided, truly was a superpower. It didn't just help you understand tears over broken toys; it helped you be a better friend, a better sister, a better human. All you had to do was be willing to put on those special glasses and look for the treasure of feeling.

"Before you judge someone, try walking a mile in their shoes.

That way, if they get mad, you're a mile away...
and you have their shoes."

Interactive Box

1. Empathy Riddles:

1. I let you feel what others do,

   If they are happy, or if they are blue.

   I'm not your shoes, but if you step in,

   Understanding and kindness will begin.

   What am I?

2. I have no eyes, but I help you see,

   The world through the heart of another than thee.

   I am a treasure, if you seek me out,

   Helping you silence anger and doubt.

   What am I?

2. Creative Exercise:

Emotion Detective Toolkit!

Imagine you're an "Emotion Detective"! Your job is to understand how someone else is feeling, even if they don't say it outright.

- ***Draw your Emotion Detective Badge!*** What does it look like?
- ***List your Top 3 Detective Tools:*** What skills or actions would you use?
- *Tool 1 (Example): Listening Ears* – To really hear not just words, but feelings too.
- *Tool 2 (Example): Observation Eyes* – To notice body language or what's happening around them.
- *Tool 3 (Example): Caring Heart Questions* – Gentle questions like "How are you feeling about that?" or "Is there anything I can do?"
- ***Solve a Mini-Case:*** Your friend Kabir usually loves art class, but today he's just staring at his paper and sighing. What "clues" would you look for, and what "Caring Heart Question" might you ask to understand his feelings?

3. Optional Visual Puzzle Idea:

Emotion Expression Match-Up

Create a two-column puzzle.

- **Column 1**: Simple drawings of faces showing clear emotions (Happiness, Sadness, Anger, Surprise, Fear, Excitement).
- **Column 2**: Short descriptions of situations that would typically cause these emotions (e.g., "Winning a race," "Losing a favourite toy," "Someone breaking a promise," "A sudden loud noise," "Seeing a big spider," "Going to an amusement park"). The child has to draw lines connecting the facial expressions to the situations that best match them, practicing how to read emotional cues and connect them to causes.

Superpower Reflection Journal Prompt:

Think about a time recently when a friend or family member was upset or very happy about something. Did you try to understand *why* they were feeling that way from their point of view? Imagine you put on "empathy glasses." What might you have seen or understood differently about *their* feelings or what that situation meant to them? How can you go on an "Empathy Treasure Hunt" next time?

Riddle Answer:

1. Empathy

2. Empathy

Chapter 9

Let It Flow, Like a River

The school auditorium was buzzing. Final round. The inter-school quiz.

Team Brainy Bunch— Aahana, Riya, Kabir, and Sara, were neck to neck trailing Team Quiz Wizards by just 2 points.

Question 1: "Which Indian river is called the 'Sorrow of Bengal' due to frequent flooding?"

Kabir buzzed confidently. "Damodar."

Quiz Master: "Correct!"

Question 2: "Which gas do plants use in photosynthesis?"

Riya tapped the buzzer. "Carbon dioxide."

Quiz Master: "Correct!"

The final question. Tie-breaker.

Question 3: "Which is the largest planet in our solar system?"

Aahana's finger moved on instinct. Buzz!

"Mars!"

The auditorium held its breath.

Quiz Master: "Incorrect. Team Quiz Wizards?"

"Jupiter," their captain replied.

Quiz Master: "Correct. That's the game!"

Aahana's heart sank. Her face flushed. The claps and cheers for the other team felt louder than thunder.

Everyone was kind–too kind. Riya said, "It happens, don't worry." Kabir offered a gentle shrug.

But Sara stayed silent. And that silence shouted louder than any words.

A few days later...

It was winter break, and Aahana had travelled to Bhubaneswar to visit her grandmother (Dadi). The moment she stepped out of the airport, she felt the difference. No biting cold. No heavy jackets or freezing fingers.

"This is what real winter feels like!" she giggled, stretching out her arms in the soft sun. "No thermals, no fog, just sunshine and guavas."

Her Dadi laughed. "That's why your Papa always says Bhubaneshwar winters are made for picnics outdoors, not pullovers and staying indoors."

The next morning, they packed a thermos of spiced chai, crispy aloo parathas, chicken sausages, aloo tikki (Indian version of hash brown), oranges, and til laddoos and headed for a picnic on the banks of the Mahanadi River, near Cuttack, just a 45-minute drive away.

As they laid out a faded but well-loved mat under a tall peepal tree, Aahana couldn't help but feel lighter. The sky was clear, the breeze was playful, a lot of birds chirped around, and the river sparkled like it was telling a hundred stories at once.

They played cards, ate slowly, and laughed easily. But as the afternoon sun leaned west, Aahana found herself quietly walking toward the river's edge, a stone in hand, her mood suddenly heavy again.

Dadi noticed.

She walked up beside Aahana and handed her a piece of orange. "Something still tugging at your heart?"

Aahana nodded slowly. "I messed up our quiz final, Dadi. It was my fault. And Sara hasn't even spoken to me properly since. I keep replaying that moment in my head. Mars. Mars. Mars."

Dadi sat down beside her on a flat rock. "You know this river, Aahana?" she said, looking at the wide flow of **Mahanadi**. "It carries so much—leaves, old branches, even people's flower offerings—but it keeps flowing. It doesn't stop to hold on to every little thing. If it did, it would become clogged, heavy, and even dangerous."

Aahana looked out at the current. A lone leaf was swirling on the surface.

Dadi continued, "Forgiveness is like this river. Especially when it's for *ourselves.* If we keep holding onto every mistake, it's like trying to dam the river with our bare hands. It just builds pressure inside us."

"But it was my mistake," Aahana whispered. "Shouldn't I feel bad about it?"

"Feeling bad is human. Carrying it forever isn't," Dadi said. "Just like this river doesn't keep the leaf forever, you can learn from it and let it go."

They sat in silence for a moment, watching the water.

"You could write to Sara, aah... sorry you kids are advanced – you just call or send a voice note," Dadi suggested while both laughed out loud. "Tell her how you felt. And also, how you feel now. That might help release some of what you're holding too."

Aahana nodded. "I think I will," and hugged her Dadi.

As they packed up the picnic, Dadi chuckled and added, "You know, your Papa once made a decision just because everyone else was doing it. Bought a fancy pair of shoes. Took him years to laugh about it. He still has the shoes, though—they pinch his feet."

Aahana laughed, imagining her dad tiptoeing in brand-new but uncomfortable shoes. "Wait... *Papa* made a mistake?"

"Oh, plenty. But he learns from them. And sometimes, those stories are the best ones to tell."

Aahana zipped her backpack, suddenly thoughtful. "Maybe it's time he answered a quiz."

Dadi winked. "Ask him something real. Something only a grown-up still growing would understand."

"Holding a grudge is like drinking poison and waiting for the other person to get sick.

It doesn't work. Just spit it out."

Interactive Box

1. Riddle of the Gentle Current:

I am not a hand, but I can help you release,

A burden of anger, and bring your heart peace.

I don't erase memories or make wrongs right,

But I wash away grudges and make your world bright.

What am I?

2. Creative Exercise:

My "Let-It-Go" Leaf Boat

Sometimes we hold onto small hurts or disappointments (from others or from our own mistakes) like heavy rocks. Let's try to let one go.

- Take a piece of paper and cut out or draw a simple leaf shape (or a little boat).
- Think of one small feeling of guilt, anger, or a grudge you've been holding onto. Write it down or draw a symbol for it on your leaf boat.
- Now, imagine a beautiful, flowing river. You can draw this river on another piece of paper.
- Place your leaf boat (with the feeling written on it) onto your drawn river. Imagine it gently floating away, carried by the current, getting smaller and smaller until it disappears.
- How does it feel to imagine letting that feeling go? What lighter, happier feeling could flow in to take its place? Draw that new feeling on the riverbank.

3. Optional Visual Puzzle Idea:

The Grudge Dam

Draw a river that is blocked by a "dam" made of rocks. Each rock is labelled with a type of grudge or negative feeling (e.g., "He ignored me," "I failed the test," "She broke her promise," "It wasn't fair"). Behind the dam, the water is shown as murky and stagnant. The puzzle is for the child to draw "release channels" or "openings" in the dam for each rock, allowing the water (and the labelled grudges) to flow out, making the water on the other side clear and fresh. They could also draw fish swimming happily in the cleared water.

Superpower Reflection Journal Prompt:

Is there a "heavy stone" of guilt, disappointment, or a grudge (towards someone else, or even yourself for a mistake you made) that you've been carrying around? Imagine you are standing by a beautiful, flowing river. What would it feel like to gently place that stone into the water and watch the current carry it away? What new, lighter feeling might you invite into your heart once that space is clear?

Riddle Answer:

Forgiveness (like a flowing river)

Section 3

Even Heroes Learn

Chapter 10

Papa's Squeaky Shoes

Aahana was back home in Gurgaon after her trip to Bhubaneswar. She still carried the calm of the Mahanadi River inside her — the kind of quiet strength that doesn't show off but flows deep.

Inspired by Dadi's advice, she decided to send a message to Sara — using Papa's phone, of course. Sara was still too young to have her own.

Sara's reply came soon after — a voice note full of giggles, forgiveness, and a very bad imitation of a quiz buzzer: "ERRRRRNT. Wrong answer, but right friend. Forgiven! I miss you. Come back soon. I've got a new Barbie House and can't wait to play with you!"

Things felt okay again. Not perfect. But peaceful.

Like rivers after a rain.

It was a chilly Saturday evening. Aahana sat at the dining table, wrapped in her favourite pink fuzzy blanket. The smell of Mom's tadka dal drifted from the kitchen. Papa was playing their favourite song — "Dance Monkey" — on the speaker while helping Mom lay out dinner.

She looked at him – calm, confident, always quick with an explanation.

My Papa is the Best, she thought. But something her grandmother had said by the river, floated back to her.

"Papa," she asked, casually, "have you ever made a mistake that you only realized much later?"

Her dad looked up from arranging the plates.

"Many," he said – a bit too quickly.

"Nooo," Aahana smirked. "Like something really silly. Like something I would do."

He smiled. "Yes. Sometimes. We all fall prey to biases, marketing lures, or just following the crowd without thinking."

Aahana raised an eyebrow. "What are biases?"

He paused. "Didn't I tell you to check the dictionary for new words?" "I'm in my blanket, ready to eat," Aahana pleaded. "Can you please help me this one time?" Papa leaned over and kissed her forehead. "All right. 'Biases' is just the plural of 'bias.' And a bias is an opinion that makes someone unfair – it bends the way they think."

Aahana laughed. "Glad I didn't check the dictionary!"

Then she added with mock surprise, "But you? You always tell me to be original and think for myself!"

"Exactly," he said, chuckling. "Let me tell you a story from a year before you were born. About a trip we–"

"No, Papa!" Aahana interrupted, eyes sparkling. "I want the shoe story! The one about the expensive sneakers."

Papa froze. "Wait... who told you about that? Was it... Mummy?" Aahana grinned. "Nooo... I won't say. Maybe it was the whispering coin!"

He laughed. "Okay, okay. Let me tell you what happened." "I was in my late 20s," he began, scooping rice into Aahana's plate. "Working in an office where suddenly everyone was talking about this new sneaker drop — white, sleek, branded, expensive... and only available in one store across the whole city."

Aahana perked up. "But Papa, which one?"

"Haha, I barely wear them now," he admitted. "But yes, they're still kept safely. I'll show you — the white ones with green and blue stripes."

"Like the ones in those glossy ads?"

"Exactly," he nodded. "Everyone at work started wearing them. They clicked pictures. They walked around differently — heads higher, steps louder. It was like the shoes gave them superpowers."

"And...?"

"And I felt left out," he admitted. "Even though my old shoes were just fine — comfortable, broken-in, reliable. I suddenly wanted what everyone else had. I didn't stop to ask myself why."

"So... you bought them?"

"Oh yes," he said. "Shiny white sneakers, with soft green and blue stripes. Way above my budget. I convinced myself they were an 'investment'."

"Were they comfy?"

"Not at all!" he laughed. "They squeaked when I walked. Pinched my toes. And once, during a Friday team presentation, I stepped forward and—squeeeaaakkk! Everyone turned to look at my shoes. Not my ideas. Not my analysis.

My. Squeaky. Shoes!"

Aahana burst out laughing. "Papa! Your sneakers sabotaged your carrier!"

He grinned. "No, no... not career, Aahana. Say it with me — kuh-reer."

"They tried," he said, still laughing. "But I learned something. I wasn't really buying shoes — I was buying belonging. I thought if I looked like everyone else, I'd be accepted more."

Aahana paused. "That... kind of makes sense."

Papa nodded. "It's okay to admire things. But when we stop thinking for ourselves, we give up something precious — our own voice."

He looked thoughtful. "Those sneakers are still in the back of my cupboard. And whenever I feel tempted to follow the crowd again, I wear them for five minutes. The squeak reminds me:

Comfort and character > Coolness."

Later that night, Aahana scribbled in her journal:

"Even Papa has a Fast Brain. Even Papa forgets to think sometimes." She smiled.

That made her feel a little more grown-up.

And her Papa?

Just a little more human.

"Flamingos only stand on one leg because if they lifted both, they'd fall over.

See? Even nature looks cool doing silly things."

Interactive Box

1. Riddle of the Gentle Current:

I wasn't too cheap,

But I made quite a squeak.

I looked like a trend,

But I pinched till the end.

I'm not just a shoe,

I'm a reminder too.

What am I?

2. Creative Exercise:

"If My Parent Had a Fast Brain Moment..."

Instructions:

We all have Fast Brain moments — even adults! Imagine a silly decision your parent might make if their Fast Brain took over. Now turn it into a fun comic panel or short story.

- What would they do?
- (Buy ten ice creams? Wear neon sunglasses to work?)
- What would their Slow Brain say afterward?
- Would they laugh? Learn something?

Now draw or write a 3-step comic strip:

1. The Fast Brain moment
2. The Oops! consequence
3. The Slow Brain realization

3. Optional Visual Puzzle Idea:

"Who's Following the Crowd?"

Create a spot-the-difference or find-the-odd-one-out scene:

- Draw a group of 6–7 characters wearing identical trendy outfits or accessories.
- In the middle, one character looks confused or uncomfortable – holding sneakers that squeak or trying on something they're not sure about.
- The puzzle: "Can you spot the one who followed the crowd... and is now thinking twice?"

Bonus twist: Let readers circle which characters look *confident vs. just copying.*

Superpower Reflection Journal Prompt:

Grown-ups don't always get it right – and that's okay.

Write about a time when someone older than you made a mistake (or admitted one).

- What did they do?
- How did they handle it?
- What did you learn from watching them learn?

If you could remind one grown-up of a lesson gently (like a squeaky shoe!), what would it be?

Riddle Answer:

Papa's Squeaky Shoes or:
A Mistake Made by Following the Crowd

Section 4

How Aahana Made Friends with her Emotions

Chapter 11

The Tear Whisperer

The living room was a mess of paper crowns, balloon strings, and half-eaten cupcakes. Aahana had just helped clean up after her cousin Arjun's birthday party. Music still buzzed faintly from the speaker. Somewhere, a toddler was giggling at a game of peekaboo gone wild.

But one person was missing from the group photo — Sara.

"She's in the guest room," Papa said softly, folding a tablecloth. "Didn't want cake. Didn't want games."

Aahana looked up, puzzled. That didn't sound like the Sara she knew.

"Want me to check?" she offered.

Papa nodded, smiling gently. "Just listen. Sometimes, that's more than enough."

Aahana tiptoed through the corridor, holding a crumpled party hat in one hand — the feather on top was flopping sideways like a sleepy bird.

She knocked once, then slowly pushed open the door.

There, curled under a faded bedsheet, was Sara. Her eyes were red, her nose was stuffy, and her whole face looked like it had been through a very rainy day.

Aahana didn't say anything.

She didn't ask, What happened? Or say, Don't cry. Or try to make jokes, even though she had some really good ones.

She just sat beside her. Quiet. Like a wind next to a window — not pushing, not pulling. Just there.

After a minute, she gently placed the floppy feather hat on Sara's head. It landed sideways. They both managed a tiny smile, like a flashlight being turned on low.

Still, Aahana didn't speak. She had learned something from her Papa: Tears don't always want answers. Sometimes, they just want space to breathe.

Minutes passed like clouds — slow and soft. ⛅☁

Finally, Sara whispered, “I didn’t like the game. They laughed when I got out first.”

She sniffled. “And I missed you last week.”

Aahana nodded. “I missed you too.”

Then she said it, very gently:

“Tears speak a language of their own. And I’m learning to understand it.”

That night, while brushing her teeth, Aahana told Papa what happened.

“You were amazing,” he said. “You were a Tear Whisperer.”

“What’s that?”

“Someone who listens to sadness... without trying to fix it right away. Someone who hears even what’s not being said.”

Aahana smiled, minty foam in her mouth.

“Sounds like a quiet superpower.”

Papa winked. “The quietest ones often are.”

“Did you know? Under a microscope, tears actually look like snowflakes.

So technically, crying just turns your face into a tiny winter wonderland.”

Interactive Box

1. Riddle of the Salty Rain:

I am a quiet rain that falls from your eyes,

Not because of clouds, but when a deep feeling lies.

Some think I am weak, a thing to conceal,

But I'm just a whisperer, helping you heal.

What am I?

2. Creative Exercise:

My "Okay to Be Sad" Care Package

Everyone feels sad sometimes, and that's okay! Create a "Care Package" for yourself (or a friend) for days when the "Tear Whisperers" visit.

- Draw a box or a pretty basket.
- Inside, draw or write down 4-5 things that can bring comfort and acknowledge sadness in a gentle way. These aren't to stop sadness, but to make it feel more manageable and understood. Examples:
- A soft, cozy blanket.
- A favourite gentle book or soothing music.
- A journal and a pen to write or draw feelings.
- A reminder note: "It's okay to cry. Your feelings are valid."
- A picture of someone you can talk to if you need a hug or a listening ear.

3. Optional Visual Puzzle Idea:

The Path of a Tear

Draw a large, stylized teardrop. Inside the teardrop, create a gentle, flowing maze or path.

- ***Start of the path (top of the teardrop):*** "A Big Disappointment" or "Feeling Very Sad."
- ***Along the path:*** Little comforting stations or words such as "A Hug," "Talking it Out," "Listening to Music," "A Good Cry."
- ***End of the path (bottom of the teardrop, where it would fall):*** "Feeling a Little Lighter" or "Ready to Heal." The idea is to show that going through the process of acknowledging sadness (the tear) can lead to relief.

Superpower Reflection Journal Prompt:

Think of a time you felt really sad but tried hard not to show it. How did that feel inside? What do you think your "Tear Whisperers" might have been trying to tell you about what mattered to you in that situation? If you had allowed yourself to acknowledge your sadness or even cry, how might it have helped you heal or connect with someone?

Riddle Answer:

Tears

Chapter 12

The Fear Fairy's Secret

Sara was vibrating with excitement. "It's here! It's finally here!" she announced dramatically at their usual weekend meeting spot in the park. She pointed towards a brand-new, incredibly tall, twisty climbing structure that looked like a metal spaghetti monster. "The 'Sky-High Serpent'! Last one to the top is a rotten space slug!" And with that, she was off, scrambling up the lower rungs like a squirrel.

Kabir, after a moment's careful inspection of the structure's base, followed at a more measured pace. Riya, ever cautious, was reading the safety instruction sign. Aahana, however, felt her stomach do a nervous flip-flop just looking at how high the Sky-High Serpent reached. A cold, prickly feeling spread through her limbs. It was Fear, and it was loud.

"Woah, that's REALLY high!" a voice screamed in her head. "What if you slip? What if a rung is loose? You could fall! Don't do it! Stay on the nice, safe ground!"

Aahana hated this feeling. It made her feel small and wobbly. Sara was already halfway up, waving like a fearless flag. Even Kabir was making steady progress. Why did she have to be the scaredy-cat?

She remembered how her dad had once told her that fear wasn't necessarily a bad thing. He'd said it was like a little alarm bell, trying to keep her safe. But right now, her alarm bell was clanging so loudly, it was deafening.

Just then, Riya finished reading the sign and came over. "It says it's built with super-strong materials and checked every morning," she reported. "Looks safe, if you're careful." She noticed Aahana's pale face. "You okay, Aahana? It is pretty tall."

"I... I don't know," Aahana mumbled, her gaze fixed on the dizzying height. "My brain is just shouting 'DANGER!' at me."

"Ah, your personal Fear Fairy is on high alert today," a voice said. It was Aahana's father, who had walked over to join them, having seen the commotion around the new structure.

"Fear Fairy?" Aahana asked, picturing a tiny, panicked fairy buzzing around her head.

Her father smiled. "That's what I like to call that protective instinct. Imagine, Fear isn't a big scary monster trying to spoil your fun, but a tiny, super-cautious Fear Fairy whose main job is to protect you and keep you safe. She flies around with a little checklist, constantly scanning for anything that could possibly hurt you."

He pointed to the climbing structure. "So, when you look at something tall and new like that, your Fear Fairy immediately shouts, 'Hold on! New situation! Potential risks! Height involved! Slipping hazard!' Her voice is loud because she really, really wants you to pay attention and not get hurt."

Aahana thought about this. It was a bit like Fear in that movie "Inside Out," who was always imagining worst-case scenarios to keep Riley safe.

"So, the secret of the Fear Fairy," her father continued, "is that she's not trying to stop you from doing everything. She's trying to make you pause, think, and be careful. Her job is to highlight the risks so you can decide if they're real and if they are, what you can do to be safe while still trying something new."

"So, when my Fear Fairy shouts about falling," Aahana said, "it's not to make me never climb, but to remind me to hold on tight and check my footing?"

"Exactly!" her father said. "You listen to your Fear Fairy's warning – that's her being helpful. You thank her for the information. Then you decide. Is the risk too big? Or can you manage it by being careful, by having a friend spot you, or by starting slowly?"

Aahana looked at the Sky-High Serpent again. Her Fear Fairy was still chattering nervously in her ear, but her voice didn't sound quite as terrifying anymore. It sounded more like a worried friend.

"Okay, Fear Fairy," Aahana thought. "I hear you. It's high. I need to be careful. Thanks for the heads-up."

She took a few deep breaths. Sara was now at the very top, cheering. Kabir was about three-quarters of the way up.

"I… I think I want to try," Aahana said to Riya and her dad. "Maybe just a little way up at first."

"Great idea," said her dad. "Go at your own pace. I'll be right here."

Riya smiled. "I'll spot you from down here if you like."

Aahana approached the structure. Her hands were a little sweaty, but she focused on the first rung. Hold on tight. Check your foot. Step by step, she began to climb. Her Fear Fairy was still there, whispering cautions, but Aahana was also listening to another voice now, a quieter one that was curious and wanted to see how far she could go.

She didn't go all the way to the top like Sara, or even as high as Kabir. But she climbed higher than she thought she would, high enough to feel a thrill of accomplishment and see the park from a new, exciting perspective.

When she climbed back down, her legs were a tiny bit shaky, but her heart was full.

"You did it!" her dad said, giving her a high-five.

"It was still scary," Aahana admitted, "but it was also… kind of fun once I got going."

She realized her Fear Fairy hadn't disappeared. She was still there, probably already scanning the park for the next potential hazard. But Aahana wasn't annoyed by her anymore. She understood her Fear Fairy's secret: her job was to help, not to hinder. And knowing that made Aahana feel braver than ever.

"Bravery isn't feeling zero fear—
it's feeling fear and doing it anyway.

(Just don't use this rule to poke a sleeping bear. Seriously. Don't.)"

Interactive Box

1. Riddle of the Helpful Alarm:

I buzz and I shout when danger is near,

My voice can be loud, filling you with unease and fear.

But I'm not a monster, trying to cause you fright,

I'm your secret protector, helping you do what's right (and safe!).

What am I?

... Fear (your helpful Fear Fairy or Guardian Alarm)

2. Creative Exercise:

My Fear Fairy's Safety Checklist & My Brave Steps!

Think of something that makes you feel a little bit scared or nervous (like trying a new food, speaking in class, or going into a dark room).

Draw your Fear Fairy! Is it tiny and cautious? Does it wear a little safety helmet?

Fear Fairy's Checklist: Imagine what your Fear Fairy is whispering to you about this situation. Write down 2-3 "safety warnings" or "potential risks" it's pointing out. (Example: For speaking in class – "What if I forget my words?" "What if others laugh?")

Your Brave Steps Plan: Now, write down 2-3 small, brave steps you can take to face this fear safely, even with the Fear Fairy's warnings. (Example: For speaking in class – "I can practice what I want to say first." "I can remember everyone feels nervous sometimes." "I can take a deep breath before I start.") Acknowledging the fear (the checklist) but then planning brave steps can make scary things feel more manageable!

3. Optional Visual Puzzle Idea:

Fear Factor Filter

Draw a scene with several potentially "scary" but ultimately manageable situations for a child (e.g., a friendly dog barking, a darkish hallway with a light switch at the end, a slightly wobbly-looking but safe small slide, a plate with a new vegetable). The puzzle is to draw a "Fear Filter" over each situation. The child then writes down:

1. What the "Fear Fairy" might be shouting about it (the perceived danger).
2. One "Brave Thought" or "Safe Action" they could use to manage that fear. Example for the dog: Fear Fairy says: "Big teeth! Loud bark!" Brave Thought: "The owner says he's friendly. I can ask to pet him gently."

Superpower Reflection Journal Prompt:

Think of something that usually makes your "Fear Fairy" sound its alarm bells. What is its protective message to you in that situation? Is the danger it's pointing out something you need to avoid completely, or is it something you could approach with a bit of caution and bravery? What's one small, safe step you could take to face that fear, even just a little?

Riddle Answer:

Fear

Chapter 13

Princess Disgust and the Boundaries Spell

Aahana was at Sara's house, along with Riya and Kabir. Sara, in a fit of adventurous creativity, had discovered a forgotten packet of neon-green food colouring and an almost-empty tub of vanilla ice cream in the freezer.

"Behold!" Sara announced, brandishing a bowl of luridly green, slightly lumpy ice cream. "I call it... Alien Slime Delight! Who wants the first taste?"

Kabir peered at it skeptically. Riya politely declined, saying she'd just had a big lunch. But Sara, with her usual persuasive enthusiasm, turned to Aahana. "Come on, Aahana! It's an adventure for your taste buds! You have to try it!"

Aahana looked at the unnaturally green concoction. A strong feeling welled up inside her – a definite "YUCK!" Her nose wrinkled. Her stomach did a little flip. This wasn't just about not liking a flavour; the colour, the texture, everything about it screamed "Do not eat!"

But Sara was looking at her with wide, expectant eyes. Aahana didn't want to hurt Sara's feelings or seem like a spoilsport. She almost said, "Okay, just a tiny bit."

Just then, she remembered a conversation she'd had with her mom about all the different emotions being like characters in her own personal "Inner Fairyland." Her mom had described Disgust not as a grumpy, negative character, but as a very particular and protective princess – "Princess Disgust."

"Princess Disgust," her mom had explained, "is like the guardian of your well-being. Her job is to protect you from things that could be harmful or 'toxic' – not just bad food that could make you sick, but also situations or behaviours that feel wrong for you, that go against your values, or that make you feel yucky inside. She's the one who helps you know when something just isn't right for you."

Aahana pictured this Princess Disgust in her mind: elegant, a little bit sassy, with very high standards, holding a delicate shield. And this princess was currently waving a big red flag about the Alien Slime Delight.

"Princess Disgust also has a very powerful magic," her mom had continued. "It's called the 'Boundaries Spell.' When she signals 'yuck' or 'this isn't right for me,' she's giving you the power to say 'no' kindly but firmly. She helps you draw a line to protect yourself and stay true to who you are."

Looking at the green ice cream, Aahana felt Princess Disgust's signal loud and clear. It wasn't about being mean to Sara; it was about listening to her own body and feelings.

She took a breath. "Sara, that's... incredibly green!" she said, trying for a light tone. "And I'm super impressed with your adventurous spirit! But you know, my tummy is a bit sensitive today, and I think this particular delight might be a bit too adventurous for me right now. Maybe Kabir is brave enough?"

Kabir, surprisingly, took the bait. "Well, I did once eat a mud pie on a dare," he mused, and took a microscopic spoonful. His face immediately confirmed all of Aahana's internal warnings. "Definitely... alien," he managed, making a face.

Sara giggled, not at all offended, and then bravely tried some herself, admitting it was "perhaps better as a science experiment than a dessert."

Aahana felt a quiet sense of relief and strength. She hadn't been rude, but she also hadn't ignored that strong "yuck" feeling. Princess Disgust's Boundaries Spell had worked.

Later that week, a similar situation arose. A new girl in class, Maya, started gossiping unkindly about another classmate during lunch. Some of the other kids were giggling along, but Aahana felt that familiar uncomfortable, "yucky" feeling rise up. Princess Disgust was waving her red flag again. This wasn't physically toxic, but it felt emotionally toxic. It felt mean.

The old Aahana might have just stayed quiet, not wanting to make waves. But remembering Princess Disgust, she decided to cast a small Boundaries Spell.

“Hey Maya,” Aahana said, her voice calm but firm. “I don’t really feel comfortable talking about other people like that. Maybe we could talk about what we’re going to do in art class instead?”

There was a moment of silence. Maya looked surprised, but then Riya chimed in, “Yeah, I was wondering if we’re going to use clay today!”

The conversation shifted. Aahana hadn’t been preachy or aggressive, but she had drawn a line, and it felt good. It felt authentic.

Aahana realized Princess Disgust was a really important ally in her Inner Fairyland. She wasn’t just about avoiding broccoli or weird-coloured ice cream. She was a wise guardian who helped Aahana listen to her gut, protect her own well-being, and stay true to her values by knowing when and how to say “no” or “that’s not for me.” Understanding Disgust wasn’t about being negative; it was about respecting herself and her boundaries.

“Your stomach has 100 million brain cells.

So when your tummy says ‘NOPE,’ listen. That’s your second brain being allergic to nonsense.”

Interactive Box

1. Riddle of the Royal Protector:

I wear a crown and wrinkle my nose,

At things that are harmful, from your head to your toes.

From spoiled, sour milk to a mean, unkind jest,

I help you say "No!" and put up a good test (of your boundaries!).

Who am I?

2. Creative Exercise:

Princess Disgust's Royal Garden of Boundaries!

Imagine Princess Disgust is the royal gardener of your "Inner Fairyland," protecting your special space.

- ***Draw a beautiful garden.*** This is "Your Authentic Self Garden."

- ***What precious "flowers" (representing your values or things you like) grow in your garden?*** Draw and label at least three. (Examples: Kindness Flower, Honesty Rose, Fun Daisy, Creativity Orchid, Respectful Friendship Tree).

- ***Princess Disgust's "Keep Out!" Signs:*** What things are "toxic" or "yucky" that Princess Disgust would want to keep out of your garden to protect your flowers? Design 2-3 funny or firm "Keep Out!" signs and place them at the edge of your garden. (Examples: "No Unkind Teasing Allowed!" "Entry Denied for Peer Pressure Pests!" "Beware: Gossip Grubs Not Welcome!")

- ***The Boundaries Spell:*** What's one kind but firm thing you could say (your "Boundaries Spell") if someone tries to bring one of those "toxic" things into your garden? Write it on a little scroll near Princess Disgust.

3. Optional Visual Puzzle Idea:

The "Yuck" or "Yum" Sorter (for physical and social situations)

Create two columns labelled "Feels Right for Me (Yum!)" and "Feels Wrong for Me (Yuck! - Thanks, Princess Disgust!)"

Provide a list of short scenarios or pictures, including:

- Eating a fresh apple.
- Being asked to share a secret that isn't yours.
- Playing a fair game with friends.
- A friend wanting you to ignore someone new.
- Wearing clothes you feel comfortable in.
- Tasting food that smells spoiled. The child has to sort these into the "Yum!" (feels good/right) or "Yuck!" (feels bad/wrong/unsafe) columns, practicing how Disgust helps identify things that cross personal boundaries or values.

Superpower Reflection Journal Prompt:

Think about a time you felt that strong "yuck" or "this isn't right for me" feeling – your inner Princess Disgust sending a signal. What was the situation? Did you listen to that feeling and set a "Boundary Spell" by saying "no" or moving away? Or did you ignore it? How did it feel afterwards? How can you honour Princess Disgust's warnings more in the future to help you stay safe, healthy, and true to yourself?

Riddle Answer:

Princess Disgust
(your inner guide for what feels wrong or yucky).